Just Like Home

Just Like Home
by Jean B. Boyce

Illustrated by Bil Keane
Creator of "The Family Circus"

International Standard Book Number
1-56684-607-2

Library of Congress Control Number
2001130938

Printed in the United States of America

Distributed by

Evans Book Inc.
805 West 1700 South
Salt Lake City, UT 84104
801-975-1315

PIQUE OF PERFECTION

Perfectionists take pains
    With everything they do—
The only problem is,
    They give a few to you!

Jean B. Boyce

JUST LIKE HOME

If the clutter in your house
    Tends to make your ego low,
Try an unexpected call—
    On most anyone you know.

SPARE THE COOK

To have a hearty meal these days
Is really not that hard,
The only thing we seem to need
Is one small credit card!

FRIDGE BENEFITS

These "fast-food days" some moms
    don't cook,
So what's the fridge used for?
For making ice and posting things
With magnets on the door.

FOOD FOR THOUGHT

When Junior crams for his exams
He burns the kitchen light,
Though drinks and snacks are plentiful,
There's not a book in sight!

DELAYED ACTION

Sound travels much slower than light,
With kids it's certainly true—
Advice that we give when they're young
Takes years before it gets through!

FRUSTRATION

The phone rings when you're showering,
    And makes you feel uptight;
Like when you're asked a question
    Just after one big bite.

DIALING DILEMMA

I dial a number—then I hear:
"Press 1, press 2, press star" (Oh dear!)
Next comes a voice that's worst of all—
"If you would like to make a call . . ."

ON OUR DOORSTEP

This fast age of travel
Promotes invitations;
Alas, we no longer—
Have distant relations!

PRIZE POSSESSIONS

Our house has a lot of antiques,
    Collectors could put on a show.
They might even treasure the things
    We wanted replaced long ago.

CAUGHT INBETWEEN

From Halloween to Christmas Eve
The merchants make it pay,
The trouble is—it seems to slight
Thanksgiving on the way.

WITH DOZENS OF COUSINS

"Thanksgiving day was fun and games,"
I wrote in my memory book.
But that was when I was <u>the child</u>—
Before I became <u>the cook</u>!

LAZY DOES IT!

The folks who first shine
      Christmas lights
Are apt to make us frown,
The reason for their
      promptness is—
They never take them down!

MIXED FEELINGS

If you give a neat present
You are sure to feel nice,
'Til the day after Christmas
When it's on for half price.

YOUNG IDEAS

OOPS!

Miss Three ate lots of Christmas treats
(The tray was full—and no one near it)
"Uh Oh!" she said, "I might throw up,
And then I'd lose the Christmas spirit!"

IN REVERSE

Kids don't think moms are inspired,
Waking 'em up when they're tired;
<u>Then</u> when they're full steam ahead
  Hustling them off to bed!

WHAT ELSE IS NEW?

Our three-year-old informs us
  In tones as smooth as silk,
That ice is made from water—
  And snow is made from milk!

SMALL EXCEPTIONS

Our children aren't perfect,
  We frequently scold,
But tax time is different—
  For once they're pure gold!

HAD IT!

"Let's go!" said a youngster
    On the chapel's back row,
"We wasted our money—
    I'm tired of this show!"

HOME BOY

They sent him to camp so he'd learn how
To make decisions—here and now!
The second day—on his own
He <u>decided</u>! He'd come <u>home</u>!

ON THE LOOKOUT

A book is fine to give
A girl too old for toys,
And one that should appeal:
Is *How to Scout—For Boys.*

OUT OF CIRCULATION

When little Suzy heard about
    a bachelor's degree,
She sighed and said, "I guess
    that means
Less boys to marry me."

BLESSINGS IN DISGUISE

It's futile to have riches,
The Bible tells us so—
And anyone with children
In college ought to know.

KEY POSITION

"All my friends get the key to the car
When turning sixteen," said our son;
So we gave him the key to the house—
To show we would not be outdone!

MAINSTAYS

"The family will stay
Together if they pray . . ."
That's been our guide so far.
Another way we've found
To keep the kids around—
Is just to own one car.

SAD TO SAY

At home our son just nods or grunts
(With words we're out of touch)
And yet he gets low marks in school
Because he talks too much.

BUDGET BUSTERS

Our teenage children think
They know what thrifty means,
They save a buck on shoes
And so they buy some jeans.

THE TRUTH IS . . .

When someone says to me:
  "How <u>did</u> you get those
    handsome sons?"
I tell them honestly—
  "Same way folks get the
    homely ones."

OFF THE RECORD

Since "39 and <u>holding</u>" means
  An age no one must know—
My son asked me how old I'd be
  If I would just <u>let go</u>!

FIGHTING ODDS

It is really a fact—
Kids keep marriage intact!
They cause such a tizzy
Keeping parents so busy,
Until couples at night
Are too worn out to fight!

AROUND AND ABOUT

BRAG AND BAGGAGE

Motor trips across the nation
Start with great anticipation,
What was lacking in perfection—
Folks "make up" in recollection!

STALLING ALL CARS

It's called the "rush hour" of the day,
Which makes no sense at all,
For that's the time—to our dismay—
When all we do is <u>crawl</u>!

WOULDN'T YOU KNOW?

The car door squeaks, the oil pan leaks,
    Front end is out of line,
But check them at the fix-up shop—
    And the darn things work just fine!

SPACE AGE

The man today who conquers space
Is he who finds a parking place!

SHAKEDOWN

An optimist is someone
Who trusts the merchant
    hawks;
Expecting to find contents
The same size as the box!

SALES PITCH

Some merchants keep us in the dark,
    (Their ads confound the brave)
Instead of stating what things <u>cost</u>,
    They tell us what we <u>save</u>!

LOOKING BACK

Our neighbor claims that college days
    Were the happiest in his life—
The only time he had between
    A mother and a wife!

THEN AND NOW

In "dorm-door" days his signs would shout:
    Knock off the war! Stamp hunger out!
Today his postups simply state—
    It's bingo night from six to eight.

CAUGHT IN PASSING

If ever you happen
    To cross her path—
She's never at a loss
    For a paragraph!

BUSY COMMUTE

At the red lights she puts on her makeup,
Does her hair on the yellow (or green);
She makes a few calls on her cell phone—
    Then a siren disturbs her routine.

HAVE YOU HEARD?

The words in print
Sometimes need proof;
But <u>whispered</u> words
We're sure are truth!

SUGAR OR SPICE

A lot could be said
   In her favor,
But <u>other</u> things—
   Have more flavor!

HARD TO FIGURE

How come when I was young
And my figure looked just great
The money wasn't there—
So the shopping had to wait?

How come in later years
When my figure isn't there
Even though the money is—
I can't find a thing to wear?

DESIGNS ON US

Designers have a reason
For making fashions strange,
That way—with every season,
We'd welcome <u>any</u> change!

HIS AND HERS

ON THE GO

Some wives today don't miss a beat!
Fresh up at dawn to set a pace
From car, to store, to school, to work,
Her ins and outs are like a race.

At close of day, the kids are fed
And tucked in bed—but mom's not through,
For while she sleeps she's dreaming up
Some projects for her <u>mate</u> to do!

MARGIN FOR ERROR

Of course no one is perfect
(On that we'd all agree)
Then why are we expecting—
The man we married to be?

SALESMANSHIP

If you want your mate to help,
    Don't coaxingly pursue it;
Just tell him at <u>his</u> age—
    He really shouldn't do it!

ENOUGH SAID

My mate and I had words,
And yet it turned out fine;
Although we both <u>had</u> words—
I kept a few of mine!

THAT COVERS IT

Men fall into three classes,
(Just ask an authority)—
The intelligent, the handsome,
And the majority!

GROCERY BASKET CASE

Check ads for price—use coupons more
   To help save money at the store;
But if you want to stay on top—
   Don't send your husband out to shop!

THAT FIGURES

In dating days—when in a crowd,
He'd grab the tab and she was proud.
They're married now, and naturally
Her views on cash are not so free.

HOLIDAY GETAWAY

When friends see the luggage we haul
   They say we have figured it wrong.
We don't "get away from it all"—
   Instead we just take it along!

TRAVEL TIPS

"Take twice the cash and half the clothes"
   (Advice you must <u>not</u> heed!)
Take <u>twice</u> the clothes—for heaven knows
   Which half you're going to need!

TEST OF TIME

Two weeks on vacation
So quickly disappears,
But two weeks on a diet
Seems more like 20 years!

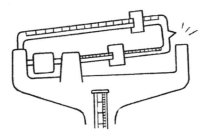

THE BOTTOM LINE

The pounds I thought I'd lost
   We're not too hard to find,
A three-way mirror check—
   And they were right behind!

MAKE 'EM HAPPY

There's no harm in flubbing,
  Now and then we <u>should</u>—
Nothing else makes <u>others</u>
  Feel so doggone good!

HUMAN NATURE

It makes a wife feel happy
And pleased with overweight
To see it on a woman—
Her husband used to date.

COUNT ON IT

When folks are young
And trim, no doubt,
They count their cash
When eating out.

In later years
When better fed,
It's the calories—
They count instead!

HEFTY HAUL

This week my mate shed 20 pounds
And I got rid of ten,
That's why we favor cleaning out
Our basement now and then.

NO LETUP—ANY SEASON

From summer weeding row by row,
We rake fall leaves—then shovel
    snow,
We put the firewood in a stack,
And work to fill old Santa's pack.
At last it's spring! Can we relax?
Not yet—it's time for income tax!

POINT OF VIEW

FROM THE BRIDE'S FATHER

It cost me a ton to get her wed!
(Could have bought 'em a house
    instead!)
So it puzzles me when people say
    That I <u>gave</u> the bride away!

NIP AND TUCK

If bills keep rolling in
He'll soon become a debtor,
Although he's doing well—
Inflation's doing better.

PREJUDICE AND PRIDE

If our darling picks a mate
We judge to be inferior—
Then how come they produce
A grandchild so superior!

THE REAL WORLD

They say—for what it is worth:
The meek shall inherit the earth;
But the meek have too much to do,
They inherit the grandkids, too!

IT WORKS

He watches sports
She likes ballet,
He stays up late
She hits the hay.

He can't stand cats
But she has two,
His type is red
And she's a blue.

And yet they cope
(No flying fur)
For she likes him
And he likes her.

BRANCHING OUT

Stepdads, stepmoms, stepgrandmas, too,
Step up and view these matters;
Today instead of family trees—
We seem to have step ladders!

WHAT NEXT?

"The check is in the mail," they say,
Or: "I've been out of town."
One more excuse we hear today—
Is: "My computer's down."

SOMEWHERE INBETWEEN

The truth in what we read these days
Is often in disguise,
But keep informed and soon you'll learn
To read between the <u>lies</u>.

SCARY POLITICS

When Halloween is over
More spooks are on the way;
They're plotting how to sway us
    Before election day.

JIFFY GENEALOGY

If you want to trace your lineage
    And you haven't got a clue,
Simply run for public office—
    Foes will dig it up for you!

THE FLIP SIDE

In politics and life
This simple truth is found:
The people who sling mud
Are certain to lose ground!

"SOMEWHERE I HEARD . . ."

It's all right to tell a secret
    (According to folks we know)
As long as you never mention
    The person who told you so.

DONOR BONERS

The Blood Drive seemed to hit a quirk,
When someone said they gave at work.
The next one said (with some distress)
    "I'll save mine—for the IRS!"

VACATION VEXATIONS

To travel can be taxing—
Requiring more than maps;
Historic sites don't grab us
Quite like the tourist traps!

CHANGE OF VIEW

When you're safe at home and bored,
Adventure sounds exciting—
But when you're in adventure's grip,
Then home seems more inviting.

STILL A SPARK

WAY TO GO

In younger days
What sounded cool?
A motor home?
A swimming pool?
In older years
Folks change a lot—
They're glad for what
They haven't got!

I ALREADY <u>HAVE</u> WINDOWS!

What house would want a mouse?
A web? (What next—a spider?)
What crazy world would want
A web that's even wider?

My mate thinks I should cope
With internet and faxing,
But I prefer my world
More homespun and relaxing.

TO THE RESCUE

The things we don't plug in
Seem obsolete—to some,
But when the power goes out
What treasures they become!

FREE AND EASY

If plane trips are hard
Don't travel out yonder,
Instead just stay home
And let your <u>mind</u> wander.

WHERE THERE'S A WILL . . .

Some folks leave wealth to their children,
   And then there's the other kind—
Who find a good way to spend it,
   Because they are sound of mind.

HEAD FIRST

Old age is in your head
(At least they say it's so)
But soon it starts to spread,
And then it's head to toe!

IT BEATS ME

It takes four rings to reach the phone,
I'm slow in many ways,
But don't you think they've speeded up
The ringing-time these days?

CLOSE ENOUGH

"You don't look one day older!"
As folks so often say,
Could mean we <u>do</u> look older—
In <u>years</u>, but not a day!

I BLEW IT!

I missed a special birthday bash!
I wrote it in my book,
And marked it on the calendar—
But then forgot to look!

STICKING TOGETHER

The older folks grow
The closer they become,
And middle age spread
Appears to help it some.

NOW LET'S SEE

At 60-plus time doesn't drag
In fact—it swiftly passes,
I find I'm spending half a day
Just looking for my glasses.

LET'S FACE IT

It just might be a blessing
When our vision begins to dim,
Our friends look as good as ever
And our mirror shows <u>us</u> less grim!

WHAT A LETDOWN

"I fell off a twelve-foot ladder,"
Said the grandpa with flippant tongue.
When the children gasped, he whispered,
"I was just on the second rung!"

ONE-SIDED BLISS

With fifty years nonstop
They're thinner on the top
And thicker in the middle.
They celebrate with pride
And still stand side by side,
Although they lean a little.

PAST TENSE?

The past <u>can</u> be altered
Without regret—
If folks haven't written
Their memoirs yet.

NOT AGAIN

If life could be lived over,
With all its breadth and length,
This much I know for certain:
I wouldn't have the strength.

OH, WELL

I thought one day I'd win a race,
Or lose some weight, or trump an ace.
But I didn't.

I often thought I'd buy a yacht
Or find my keys, or solve a plot.
But I didn't.

I even thought I'd write a book,
Or catch a fish, or learn to cook.
But I didn't.

I thought I'd find a clever way
To end this verse before today.
But I didn't. Oh, well.